T0146816

YESTERDAY, TODAY & TOMORROW

Based on a
TRUE STORY

MARYAM FADHEL ABDULRAZAQ

authorHOUSE®

AuthorHouse™ UK
1663 Liberty Drive
Bloomington, IN 47403 USA
www.authorhouse.co.uk
Phone: 0800.197.4150

Published by AuthorHouse   04/21/2016

ISBN: 978-1-5246-3272-4 (sc)
ISBN: 978-1-5246-3307-3 (hc)
ISBN: 978-1-5246-3271-7 (e)

Characters

NOTE: CHARACTERS ARE TRUE,
BUT HAS DIFFERENT NAMES.

- Jade: My youngest sister which is 10 years old, she really likes to annoy other people but is really kind-hearted.
- Beth: My eldest sister who is 18 years old, she likes to be bossy as usual.
- Zedd: My cousin, the daughter of my dad's brother, she likes to give orders to her sisters and is 16 years old.
- Helen: Zedd's eldest sister which is 19 years old.
- John: which is also known as Jay, he is the son of my dad's sister who lives outside the country.
- Linda: My dad's cousin but is 14 years old, she lives in Qatar.
- Mathew: Linda's youngest brother, 12 years old.

- Harry, Charlie, Chris: Three brothers which are the children of my dad's cousin.

- Angelina and Victoria: the sisters of harry, Charlie and Chris, they are diamonds.

- Daniel: My handsome friend that I love everything in him he is two years younger than me, I really admire him and he is a guy that I can really count on.

- Jake: My sweet friend that never makes me sad he is in the same age of Daniel, very talkative to but he makes me smile.

- Mike: My amazing friend that I used to get annoyed from but he is warm-hearted.

- Brooke: My crazy sister that my mum didn't brought, I love this girl like a maniac and I would do anyone just to see her happy.

- William: My friend that my parents and I love and he is the kindest person I have ever seen.

- Drake: My friend that I can't live without, not anyone can understand him, but I do.

- Zack: My friend who.... I don't know what to say about him but he helped me in my life.

- Kate: My best friend that stood beside me through my ups and downs, I really love her.
- Joseph: I don't really know him but he is my friend and always wants to act cool.
- Samantha: My friend since 9 years, I really don't know what I would do without her. She is my other half.
- Becky: My Pakistani friend that is damn beautiful and is very generous.
- Manny: My classmate that really used to irritate me.
- Lloyd: My classmate that I never understood him.
- Julie and Julia: Egyptian twins that were my bus mates and my classmates, I LOVE them into pieces.
- Bella: My dad's cousin that really used to love me.
- George Michael: My hero, heart, soul, everything, My DAD.

THIS BOOK IS DEDICATED TO:

MY LOVED ONES

AND

MY LIFE; MY PARENTS

SPECIAL THANKS TO:

MY PARENTS

MY SISTERS

MY FRIENDS

AND MY ENTIRE FAMILY

Contents

Acknowledgement

I want to start with to thank my parents for the encouragement, love and support that they gave me towards writing my story and in publishing it and even my best friend Fatima Kamaluddin for being by my side through writing and helping me. All of my family and friends were a part of encouragement and a part of my story and I thank my publishing company Author House for the great opportunity in enabling me to publish my book and helping me through everything that I need in making my book a success.

Introduction

Bullying can leave a huge impact in someone's life, it may sound that it's not much of a big deal but being able to experience that every day of your life is what I have written at the beginning of the story, maybe from this chapter you will be able to see how bullying a person can really hurt them and affect them physically and emotionally. At first my intention wasn't to write a book it was just journals but then I combined them and made them a book! As you start a new chapter new interesting things come up and you will won't stop reading.

AUTHOR'S NOTE

As every moment passes and something happens in my life, I run off to the computer and type it down, every single thing that has happened to me since the age of 6 till now, every interesting part of my life. Why did I type the story of my life? It is because writing helps me to forget every bad thing that has happened to me and writing is truly my passion, whenever I'm down or upset, writing is my cure. The characters are all true but has different names, everything is true in this book except for some paragraphs that I have added, I made it more catchy and it is what I wished would really happen. The reason that I published my book wasn't for fame, the reason was to achieve something great in my life, it was my dream to publish a book. Faith, hope and patience; these are the three things that made stronger and accept life as it is.

CHAPTER 1

My Life as the Bullied Girl

I'm always the girl who gets hurt emotionally every year of the school, I'm not sure if it's from me or from the fake friends that I choose, this intimidation started while I was in grade2, I know I was young, but it was a stupid thing, there was this girl named Anne; everyone used to hate her in class because she used to pee in her pants. I don't hate her; she's my classmate and I don't Hate people.

One day, Anne came to me and told me, "Do you hate me?"

"No, of course I don't", I answered smiling.

My friends were ahead of us and heard me telling her that I don't hate her, they got pissed off, so they dragged me to the corner and started thrashing me so critically, one of the girls ran to the principle and told him that I hate them and offended their feelings, the principle spoke to me and I wasn't even attentive, because it was all falsehoods. I just said ok and rushed back to class, from that day onwards they started bullying me and hating me and kept on throwing ruthless hurtful words on me, that really hurts my feelings and I started to dislike them for doing that, I never thought that my own friends would do that to me, I thought they will be there for me, but unfortunately not, I still dislike them for what they have done to me. Consequently this maltreatment continued to the end of the year, my mum thought of changing my school for some cause, I couldn't say no to her and plus it was better for me to get fresh friends and start a new page in a new school, I really wished that my new school would be better.

Here starts the first day of grade 3, as usual my mum walked me to class on the first day and I took a seat in class gently while everyone remained staring at me like an alien just approached to class. They kept on questioning what my name is, but I kept on staring at them. I'm the shyest person in the family, I'm not social. So, this delightful girl Jane came up and started a conversation with me. I felt relaxed with her and started to chitchat with her we kept on playing paper games and she introduced me to her best friend Annabel; she's a nice kid too. I liked them a lot, by time they became my best friends and she showed me the school and where to go during recess and stuff. Well, grade 3 went on normally, at grade 6, here started the bullying all over again. I don't get it why do I always get bullied, there was this problem occurred in class and the coordinator kept on asking us what happened, every man jack lied and I was truthful about what happened. So, one day one of my friends Dana got furious because I said the truth so she said for the whole class not the talk to me. I regretted that I said the truth…but it's too late right now, the bullying of this year has already started.

The following morning, I was terrified to enter the class because everyone hates me right now and it's an unpleasant feeling to get inside a room occupied with haters. I got inside the classroom with my head facing the floor and sat down on my seat. I could hear the boys behind mocking me. I ignored them and they kept on bothering me for the whole day. I couldn't handle it anymore, I just wanted to go home and end this year. I got sick and tired of these problems and the unwise fake friends that I make every year. This continued for practically a month and then "the queen of the class" Dana decided to forgive me *as if I care*. Done, here the problems ended, but it's just the beginning of the bullying in my life.

Grade7, I thought that this year would be the greatest year, but I was mistaken at the first semester it was great, I got a wonderful friend that treasured me a lot and so did I. But you know sometimes when you are pissed off you say words you don't mean and you can't take it back once you said it, I said a cruel word to my best friend Juliet, which is now my ex-best friend. I really didn't mean it, but she has the full right to get mad at me and not talk to me but she doesn't have the right to tell the complete class not to talk to me, that hurts you know... it's not right to do that, I even told her sorry but she didn't accept it. It's her choice, at least let her break the drama and move on as if nothing happened, she kept on doing stupid stuff every day to me and it was like 19 on 1, it's not rational. I've unexploited my whole entire year crying of these senseless problems that she's causing, she's just a tot and acting immature.

I couldn't handle it, and I told my mum, she understood and spoke to her politely but that didn't work, by the time we wanted to sort out the problems but this little jealous brat came and wrecked everything and it got worse, she just wanted Juliet for herself. So the year almost ended and nothing altered. This problem continued till grade8, here where I got really worn-out of problems and bullying. I just wanted to scream "ENOUGH!"

In grade 8, we got into separated class *thank god*but complications were happening throughout recess and the jealous girl Rosie kept telling Juliet rumors about us and telling her things that we didn't even say, this girl is despised by everybody in class because of her arrogance. My friend Nicole hated Juliet too, and we had the same problems. So Rosie told Juliet things that we didn't say and started playing with fire, a lot of drama ensued this year and immature people started bantering but we didn't care and ignored them, it continued till the end of the year *TIRED OF ALL THIS*

The last year, grade 9 unfortunately Juliet is my classmate again. I didn't want problems this year because this year is the most essential year of my life. I have to focus on my studies, some minor problem happened that I ignored and didn't overhaul and I hope this is where all the bullying of my life ends.

CHAPTER 2

My Life as a Senior Girl

Since all that I've been through, I still am a tough person and I never gave up. I ended my 9th grade with many motivating and cherished memories; I got revenge from the person who tried to take an essential part of my life. Well, I almost lost one year of my life by failing in mathematics, and I have done two re tests and however failed, I'm just not involved in mathematics, but at last the principle gave me one more chance to do another re-test and I passed with acceptable results. I've always hated mathematics and set aside this phrase in my mind "failure leads to success". Anyone would be reading this would say that I'm a careless person who doesn't take caution of her schoolwork but I have my own explanations there's something inside me that no one knows about and I would never show it.

So, let's start with the first day of me being a senior (Oh yea on my first day I didn't know that failed in my re-test), I walked inside the class confidently that now I'm in the 10th grade, but everyone was staring at me as if I don't belong here, I sat on my seat and the sir told me if I have met the coordinator, I replied "no, I haven't seen her, and she's not in the block either" I was a bit worried but I let it go, as usual I like to stay quiet at the beginning few hours of the period, at break time is here where I get my energy because I get to meet my best friend and start chatting and updating each other, while we were at the break hall, my English teacher came and tapped my shoulder and told me in a sad voice, "how are you? Are you okay?", I replied, "yea I'm fine", why would she ask me, I'm fine do I look like I have a broken leg, or is there a bandage on my head, then Zedd my best friend told me that this morning she asked her about me and told her that your friend Meme failed the year, but I said no, the office called my dad and said to him that I passed unless, I wouldn't have come to school today (because it was the second day of school, but for me it was the first day)

When I came back to class my best friends William and Drake asked me, "Did you pass?"

I replied in a confused way, "Duuh, then why am I here"

After a couple of minutes someone came and told that I've been called to see the coordinator, she told me go to the office to get your results, while I was on my way to the office my heart started beating faster and faster and a lot of things were wandering inside my head, I went inside and asked for my results, it was inside a sealed envelope written "To Mr. George Michael", I arrived inside the class and sat on my bench glaring at the envelope terrified to open it, while Drake and William were staring at me fretfully, I unsealed it, I saw my grades, my eyes started to fill with tears … I sobbed, they knew that I failed, I whispered to my friend Kate with tears dropping on my cheeks "I failed", she hugged me and told me that everything will be all right . I went to the coordinator and asked her to call my mum, I needed her to come and pick me up and didn't want to stay here anymore, but she didn't reply she was asleep…

At that point I had to stay at school. I was sitting in the corner of the class, crying whenever I think of that I just lost a year of my life, I let down my friends, my cousins that had faith in me that I would pass, my parents… I didn't know how I would tell them that I failed AGAIN. The sir was explaining and I had no interest, William asked, "Why aren't you writing the notes down", I replied sadly, "why should I note them down when I don't even belong here". He didn't know what to say and gave me a nice smile and walked away. The sir noticed that I had no interest so, he asked me to answer a question, I was staring at the table, with blurry eyes, I said, "I don't know the answer", he came up to me and saw me crying and told me not·don't be scared, I wiped my tears and he explained to me the question . So typically, my first day of 10th grade was a nightmare and thank god I'm done with this year.

What I can say that grade 10 was the most exciting year. I got close to many people that I never thought would be my friends. I had many people hating me the past couple of years, but I was just an innocent girl who had nothing to care about, but now I started to love my life and understood the meaning of life, I had some certain people who were always there for me and stood beside me through my hardest times. I just couldn't describe my love to them, I used to make personalized cards to them, describing what I love about them and what they mean to me, but it's just not enough, I love my friends more than I even love myself…

Grade10…

There are many things that happened like, sports day; its right that my best friend didn't come, but I stayed with my classmates. William brought his friend and introduced us to her and I sat with her and I liked her, I usually hate meeting new people but she was nice. Her name was Therese. I was participated in relay race and I really wanted our team to win but unfortunately we didn't we won the third place, we could have won if the girl at the race line ran when the guy had blown the whistle, I guess she was not ready or something it's alright, that happened to me once. I really cried when I knew that we didn't get the 1st or the 2nd place, I don't know why but I guess that I really wanted to come back home with a medal hanged over my neck. Then when Therese saw me crying she hugged me that was so cute. when it was home time, I told my bus mates about what happened, Mohammed gave me his medal and told me, "take it, I don't need it", I was like, "Aww thanks". At least I came back home with a medal, I know it's not mine but It will be a memory to be remember.

National day of Bahrain celebration; we had to wear white and red, but I on purposely wore fully black, I was wearing my Metallica shirt with black jeans and my leather jacket, I just didn't feel like wearing white and red (: anyways I was almost the whole time with 11th graders which I literally call them my days makers, I just sat with them while they were fooling around and I was hiding in the corner of the class, well of course hiding from the co-coordinator from seeing me because she would kick me out and send me to my class, but she caught me and yelled at me, but I kept on going there, I sat with Zack watching the other crazy people playing paper football (it's a ball made out of paper and scotch tape), well Zack was very sick that day so I made sure that he doesn't get any worse and made him company, we were just talking for hours and it just felt like a couple of minutes, I just wished that day wouldn't end.

English week; OMG, this day was the worst day of 10th grade, it was awful but remarkable, English week is a specified week for the students and teachers to be gathered at the multi-purpose hall and the students should prepare anything like presentations or speeches about English, so I heard that we could sing, and I said why not give it a second shot, but alone this time, I've already sang in front of everyone in 9th grade and it was flop show(:,anyways I decided to sing demons by imagine dragons, I just had a couple of days to learn the whole song and prepare myself, I knew a couple of days wouldn't be enough to learn the entire song but I just gave it a try, the moment I went up the stage and watching at the people staring at me, my legs starting shaking so bad but I hoped no one noticed, I started to sing it was a not bad beginning but as I reached to the chorus boom ... and blank, I forgot the lyrics of the song, Kate was trying to help me remember it, but she didn't know the lyrics, I stopped and went down the stage, when I almost reached to my seat, Meme Akbar from 9th grade told me, "you sounded like a mini Adele" I gave a smirk and sat down at my seat with my blurry eyes, I wiped my tears, and started remembering myself how stupid I was to sing in front of the whole block AGAIN. I can sing but it's just that when I sing in front of many people my voice gets shaky and I sound like a squeaky frog. I should have listened to Zack, I was rehearsing in the hall and he was listening, but my voice wasn't clear enough because I was supposed to sing duet with some 8th graders singing the same song, I didn't like it so I wasn't singing properly, so when I was done, I went to him and asked him in a sarcastic way, how was my voice, he said that if u sang in front of me one more time I'm going to laugh at your face.. That was rude, but I didn't care because he's always like that with me.

End term party; WOW! The most amazing part of the year, Drake Kate, William, Joseph everyone! I really had fun, that day really can't be defined I was totally worn-out and I haven't slept the whole night and that made me even more hyper, I was literally dancing in the hallway and singing talk dirty – Jason Derulo. Drake, William and I couldn't stop chatting even if there's nothing to talk about, we hit each other, and the moment when the photographer came and took a picture of us, I hope I can get the picture and stick it on the wall of my room, that day was just special.

My dearest friends are leaving the school, I should have left but I had to stay. Vanessa, William, Zack, Kate those people who brought life to the school, I really don't know what we would do without them. 10th grade has many loveable memories and every memory will be cherished my whole life, they made my smile and they made my life perfect.

CHAPTER 3

Summer Holidays

AUGUST IS LIKE THE SUNDAY OF SUMMER! Finally!! Its summer time, I've been waiting for this holiday since a long time, we had a lot of pressure on us, and we had to study everyday so hard just to get good grades in our IGCSE exam. They had been scaring us for the whole two years that it's going to be hard and you have to study very well that it's not a normal exam that we can have fun the whole year and then study the night before the exam. Thank god it was not that hard, we all studied and did our best, we were studying in groups and explaining to each other the things that we didn't understand because all of our teachers were busy or sometimes we had to stay after school because the school ends at 2:30pm and our exam starts about 5:00pm or sometimes 4:00pm, well it depends.

We usually love to spend our free time with our cousins, since now that we have two whole months, we'll be 24/7 together. We have cousins that live in Qatar, Linda and Mathew and our relationship is very strong so they decided to stay with us the whole summer, will this holiday get any better?

When Linda and Mathew first arrived to Bahrain they came over to our house and when we first saw them we hugged them so tight it has been such a long time we haven't seen each other, so we sat down and started chatting and after a while Mathew wanted to play ps3, we joined him we played Call of duty: Black ops 2 that's the only game that we loved to play together we get so tensed and hit each other when the other wins but of course in a teasing way. Our summer together had been a lengthy one with many ups and down but it's alright no one can live a perfect life, right?

We have never been too close with our cousins like we barely say hi and that's it, my father's family is a HUGE one! So Linda and Mathew's mother is the daughter or my father's uncle, so you see … everything is mixed up and confusing so it's alright if I call them as our cousins. So this summer we got close to Harry, Charlie and Chris (their sisters Angelina and Victoria have a close relationship with us even with our parents), but the most Harry because he was always with Ali and they used to come over a lot, the most thing we used to do is play ps3 that's the most thing that took our time or sometimes we play dumb charades or just sit outside with some music played by one of their phones. One of the days, my dad got a message from Victoria telling that she's going to get engaged my reaction was mixed up I was happy for her and I felt like crying and then thought that there will be no more Victoria she will be busy with her fiancé and we can't see her like we used to . I didn't want to cry in front of everyone so I just stayed quiet. Victoria is like my eldest sister some times when I need something like an advice or someone to go to, I have her. At least she's mature and she knows what's right and what's wrong, she's just amazing person with a unique personality she might be 23 but to me she's like a young girl who lives her life the right way in an awesome way.

Engagement day!!

I thought of not getting too fancy so I just kept light makeup and wore my Abaya and got ready. It's only a 15 minutes car distance from here till their house, so when we reached, she opened the door for us and I tried not to cry until she hugged me and I exploded, when she hugged me I felt like oh my god she's not leaving us right...she was so beautiful with her pretty navy blue dress and her smile that's always drawn on her face. I just sat down staring at her laughing so gorgeously, I love seeing her happy, and that's make me happy too.

Rules for a Happy Marriage:
1. *Never be both angry at the same time.*
2. *Never yell at each other unless the house is on fire.*
3. *If one of you has to win an argument let it be your mate.*
4. *If you have to criticize, do it lovingly.*
5. *Never bring up mistake of the past.*
6. *Neglect the whole world rather than each other.*
7. *Never go to sleep with an argument unsettled.*

8. *At least once every day tries to say one kind or complimentary thing to your life's partner.*

9. *When you have done something wrong, be ready to admit it and ask for forgiveness.*

10. *It takes two to make a quarrel, and the one in the wrong is the one who does the most talking.*

I just felt like sharing this, of course everyone wants to have a happy marriage☺.

Nothing much happen and this day so the other day we went I wore my long floral dress with my tiffany blazer and heels. The moment I saw Victoria my heart raced and I just looked at her in her white dress :') damn… I really wished her all the best in her life and I wished that her fiancé would treat her like a queen among his arms. When you tell me describe Victoria, I get stuck not knowing from where to begin, and the words won't come out from my mouth. The party was amazing they were singing and the most sensational moment was when her mother stood in front of her singing and clapping while the others were singing along, the way that they were both looking at each other was unbelievable…you could see the love in their eyes. Then later on we went inside the living room with Harry, Charlie and Mathew.

We had so much fun that we didn't want to leave, so we asked Victoria if could we sleepover at their house she was fine with it but the hard part is our parents after 10 minutes of wishing that they would say yes, they finally allowed us to stay but with one condition that we'll come back home when we first wake up. We were ok with it because we were thinking of staying awake until morning. We sat and played some games, we sang because there was a mic and speakers. We really had fun it was the best sleepover we ever had, it's not like the others that we had, we were all around each other and none of us had mobile phones, if we did each one of our heads will be stuck in front of the phone till we get tired and get to sleep, that what happens with our other cousins Helen and Zedd.

After a couple of days, we went over to their house and bought ribbon sprays and fire-crackers, until we all gathered we went outdoor and started scattering ribbon spray on one another's face and bursting the fire crackers on their feet. When we were through, we realized that we made a massive chaos and we got shouting from Linda's uncle that we messed up his car with ribbon spray. Dude! It'll flutter away with the wind why should you make a big deal about it?? We didn't care and laughed about what happened. It became late-night and it was time to go back home, our parents came to pick us up but Linda's grandmother insisted them to come inside for a while, so we planned that tomorrow they'll have dinner at our house they just have to take the approval from our parents, before we leave they all went and took permission and they said yes. We were excited to have them on dinner.

On august 3rd, *"Its ma birthday, its ma birthday, imma spend ma money"*

03-08-1999... The day that I was born. I just love this day, everyone does right?? I decided to Amwaj, lagoon with my cousins Linda and Mathew but Mathew didn't want to come because his cousin from Qatar came so he stayed home with him. I got fancy wore some makeup on and left. So we decided to go to laser tag, we had the time of our lives! We really had fun, I just felt as if I was playing Call of duty: black ops in real life! When we came back home, my mum and my uncle got me a cake and full of presents were waiting for me on the table!! My cake was from dairy queen it was Oreo and vanilla ice-cream yummy. I got everything that I wanted and more... Alhamdulillah.

One morning, it was 1:00am Beth and I were singing before getting to bed, Beth got thirsty so she went to get some water from downstairs. Suddenly she entered the room took her abaya and looked like her heart was rushing! I asked her, "What's wrong????"

"Just get ready and come down!!" she answered ghastly.

I wore my abaya and went down I saw my dad crying as hell... I kept my hands on my heart; many things came up to my mind...

"Dad...what's wrong?" I asked in a sorrow voice

He said with tears falling on his cheeks, "Bella passed away"

My heart raced...*in my thoughts- no... No!!! Not Bella! How?? Nothing was wrong with her! She was just fine before going to Iran! How could this happen?!*

We hopped in to the car on our way to my dad's uncle house, and I started remembering every moment I had with her, she was just like my second mother, we were so close together. I couldn't believe that one day will arrive and I will be there in here funeral, after 2 days when they brought her body to Bahrain to bury it. We woke up early morning at 8 to go to her funeral, it was terrifying it was so crowded so we stood outside by we I mean; Beth and I. It was very hot and sunny and we didn't eat anything before leaving the house. After hours of sitting outside, Beth said come lets go and see her before they burry her. We entered and I felt like something jammed my heart and felt out of breath. My eyes were filled with tears and I couldn't stop crying, when I saw her... damn she was very beautiful mash-a-Allah [1]and she was smiling too! My heart is beating slower and slower while typing this chapter...

I miss her..

---

[1]   Saying this word to the beauty of god's creation

CHAPTER 4

Learn From Your Mistakes

NO.... I never thought I would repeat grade 10 again! And no! I'm not a failure... I'm not a loser neither a careless person! I got low marks in my IGCSE and my school didn't allow lower than C grade. I went to many schools to register for 11th grade but I was too late. My only choice was to repeat 10th grade or …. Nothing. That was apparently my only choice. Every day I had to cry, not ever laugh, and in a total frustration.

As I said in the first chapter that I always had this motto in my head; failure leads to success. I really believe in that I never let myself down and say that I can do it.

FIRST DAY OF GRADE TEN FOR A SECOND TIME...

I went the second day of school because I was afraid to go at the first day, just like what happened at my first grade 10. My heart aches when I start to remember how much I have been through… I tried to stay strong; my biggest fear was to repeat a year of my educational life. At my vacations, I couldn't wait for the first day of school, I was too excited to see my friends and all gather up in the same class again… have some fun and study in groups just like how we used to. But now everyone left school because the same thing has happened to them but I was too late and stayed in this school, while all of them left and are currently enjoying their grade 11 while I'm repeating my grade 10. Where were we? Yea, my first day of grade 10, before I entered the class we had to meet the principle by 'we" I mean my dad and I. he asked me are u satisfied with repeating the year and stuff I was just nodding my head and agreeing with everything he says because I had no choice. Everybody thought that I was fine with everything, but I wasn't. Seriously, who would be fine with it??. Then when we got out of his office my dad embraced and my eyes were filled with tears but I forced myself not to cry because I didn't want him to worry about me. Ms. Natalie was just by the gateway so she took me to my class; she opened the door and told me where my bench is. It's like grade 10 is recapping itself all again, the same thing happened they were staring at me just like an alien entered the class. I sat there talking to myself; "Meme, what did you do?" "They are my friends, but I never thought I would be in the same class as they are" "what a good launch to a dreadful year" I wondered how they are, like in class and stuff. But you know what was the interesting part is? My best friend is in the same class as I am! The first month I was damn silent in class but then later on I got used to the class, I got to know them better and know their personalities whose good and who's bad and cocky.

Let me tell you about this guy in my class who is funny and silly at the same time, his name is Lloyd, he's like the joker of the class he continuously tries to make everyone laugh and makes a fool out of himself and yes the other guy, Manny. OMG! This guy... I really don't know what to say about him, during the teacher's lecture if he didn't say the word "repeat" more than 3 times then there's something wrong with him today! He irritates me somehow.

One day, our English teacher Ms. Emily wanted to know more about us she was asking us about our likes and dislikes, when she came out to know that I LOVE writing poems and stories she asked me read one but unfortunately I don't learn any of my poems and I didn't have one with me either. So I the next day I went to her and told her if I can read my poem at class and she was looking forward to it. So when she asked the class to be quiet and told them that I'm going to recite a poem, my heart raced... I stood in front of the class with the paper in my hand and I started reading, I really don't know if they noticed my legs, paper and my voice trembling. I wrote a poem about something that just happened to me, I lost a person who is no longer in my life and it really hurts me to mention it so I wrote a poem about it for my future book of poems. I'm used to write everything that happens to me I can't continue my life without writing poems.

I even got 2 new best friends from grade 9; Jake and Mike. These two guys are the most adorable friends. On field trip day our school took us to a mall to watch a movie "the maize runner" the movie is damn good I really loved it. So after watching the film we were wandering around, Kate, Becky and I were window shopping and after that I wanted to play billiards but Kate and Becky didn't want to because they were not a fan of billiard they went bowling instead . I found Mike there so I offered him to play with me, I went to pay and took our table, he was like I'm going to beat you down and stuff =)).

We kept on playing and I really had fun with him, we kept on playing for one hour.

Okay here's another thing that happened, Remember Jake?

This guy... I used to hit him a lot but in a playful way, so once we were hitting each other in our block's hallway and he unexpectedly pushed me into the wall, the sound of my chin hitting the wall was like an A4 register falling. I felt unconscious for a while I didn't even know who assisted me to get up. I hurried to Kate, I touched my chin because it was burning me and all of a sudden, my chin was bleeding and it literally got opened I freaked "BLOOD" My biology teacher rushed me to the nurse and applied alcohol on the wound and kept a bandage. I wanted to laugh so badly but I couldn't because the scar would get bigger. As soon as I reached home my mum saw my chin and she said, "What happened? What's wrong?" she got frightened a lot I removed the bandage and showed her she straight away woke up my father from his nap and took me to the hospital, while I was walking, the people were staring at me they made me feel like as if I forgot to wear my pants.

As days went by normally our 1st unit test started and I knew that that I didn't do my best and I got bad marks, so our coordinator came into our class to tell us our marks *That's the day after the parents teacher meeting* she wanted to show everybody how we did in our exam, when she came to my name she kept on under-estimating me and showed to everyone that I am a loser and that I am repeating the year and still haven't improved my grades, that's made my mood to zero she really hurts me and made me ask myself if am I failure or not? Why is she doing this? Why is she embarrassing me in front of the whole class? That's not right she could have talked to me in private and tell me my own issues not spreading the whole thing to my class which I considered them as total strangers because I never knew them right and I never even had a conversation with any of them. So Samantha and I decided to prove her wrong, on our 2nd unit test we will show her that we are not who she thinks we are, we can be the best in class and now it's time to show her and we really did, we brought remarkable marks in our 2nd test that we were so proud of it but you know, she didn't even say a word to us because we nailed it, we didn't make a flop show just like the others.

At the end of the month of December we went to a field trip to City Centre mall to watch the penguins of Madagascar, this time Kate didn't come with me so I went with my classmates. Eva was me with me the whole time, she's my best friend's sister and now she's in my class, she's an amazing talented girl. First, Eva and I were searching for Matt because he has her phone and she wants to take it from him and now we should search all over the mall to find him, we were exhausted. Later on, when we found him we went for shopping and then we felt hungry we went to Mc Donald's, I'm a type of person; if I don't eat and feel hungry my whole body shivers and I can't stop shaking I can't even walk so, I wanted to play billiard so I went and paid and played with my friend Daniel, at first when I held the queue I couldn't hold it still and couldn't aim I felt so frustrated and stupid I played a couple of turns and then I couldn't handle it, I stood aside I almost fainted I cried and I was hoping Daniel didn't see I gave the queue to my friend and walked away.

CHAPTER 5

Look forward, Think positive

First term has ended, finally. At the first day of second term, I felt like the first day of 10th grade all over again. I have no clue why I have felt this, I entered the class and all of a sudden I started to feel sizzling and started to sweat. Why? I don't really know. Maybe it's because after a lengthy term break I came back and felt like that but that still confuses me. I really had a problem sitting in this class but now while I'm writing this it makes me think that these people had made my year and made me forget that I'm repeating the year. I used to go through some situations that I felt like something deep inside me is telling me, "you don't even belong here, look what you have done to yourself". It may not be a big deal for anyone else but for me it is. I have gone through psychological issues and I have overcome it. At second term, I did a lot of things that made me really happy. There is a girl at 9th grade who I disliked her attitude and personality and the way that she used to show off with her body. She's a kid who's acting like her shoe size and searches for attention from every single guy. Well, at the beginning of the year we had a minor fight, she used to talk behind my back to her classmates and tell ruthless stuff about me and my mother, a guy from her class came and told me and I really got pissed off I wanted to fight with her the following day but I have no idea how the coordinator found out that I was going to hit her at sports period, but before that she made her "temporary" boyfriend talk to me as if he's trying to solve things out, dude? What does it have to do with you? Why are YOU interfering? You are just a temporary boyfriend and you're trying to defend her? I thought that it's just the beginning of the year let me leave her alone and she will see what I'm going to do to her later on. So, before sports day, some girls of my class had a problem with her and I got thrilled about the problem they were really frustrated with her and her bossy-like-attitude. I got a flashback of grade 9 and what I have done to that girl that I tried to take revenge, this time I am going to play a smart game. After our march-past practice, they had a library period so I took a red marker from one of her classmates and waited until all of her class went out and straight away went to her place and wrote stuff on her bag, my aim of this thing was to see her cry and get hurt I don't mind if she said hurtful words to me but why the hell would you talk about my mum in that dirty way? I took my revenge and sat in class with a huge smile on my face and I definitely saw her cry and pissed off. But later on she took her bag and gave it to the coordinator and said that she guess that I did it because everyone knows I take paybacks in my own way. They took my English notebook while I was away and tried to look if my handwriting is the same as the handwriting in her bag, but I have many handwritings, I can fake it really good. But then they called me to the coordinator and the student counselor was there, her bag was on the table and I wanted to laugh. The student counselor yelled at me and I really didn't give a shit because I don't care what punishment she's going to give me and what saying she wants to say to me. I'm happy of what I did and nothing can change that. The coordinator let me to write that I'm not going to do that again and why have I done that. After that I went to break and some girls came and told that she's searching for you and she's really heated. She made me laugh I swear, what do you want to do? Hit me? I will break your head if you even touch me, I may look thin but you have no idea that I could send you right away to the hospital. After 2:30 I was on my way to the bus and I saw her in front of me, Samantha told me, "put a big smile on your face and you will put her on fire". I smiled and she gave me a stupid smirk, I turned and told her, "if you really want to fight come here and I will break your head!! Don't run away!!" She actually got scared and went, she only did that because she was with her boyfriend and wanted to show off. This term is where I got used to my classmates but not 100%. The things that made me happy at school is these three people; Jake, Mike and Daniel. I can't really describe these amazing angels, by just seeing them every day makes my day and seeing them smile towards me makes me feel lucky that I have them in my life. We had a field trip and they made us decide to where we should go, some of them decided to go to a resort but half of them didn't accept so I thought of going to "Funland" which is a skating arena and it's the only skating arena in Bahrain. We asked 9th graders they were fine with it actually very excited, which that drew a smile on my face. Day by day I couldn't wait for Thursday to arrive. When we were in the bus on our way to Funland and Indian music was played while all of us were chatting taking selfies, our class teacher told us that we are boring and gave us a non-interested face, "Excuse me? We are boring? I will let you to take back your words" I replied with a smiling face. Linda and I stood up and asked the driver to pump up the music and danced like drunken people despite the fact that everyone were clapping, laughing and taking videos of us. We really had fun and once we reached Funland, I ran to the gate and waited for them and everyone chuckled at me. As soon as I entered and wore my skating shoes I was the first one to enter the rink and everyone stared at me in a shocking way and wandering how do I know how to skate that good. A 7th grader entered the rink and had difficulty in skating so I took his hand and helped him to skate but he literally had no balance and fell, I was laughing so bad and apologized and left. As quickly as they opened the blue lights I wore my striped orange neon jacket and I was glowing. Music was on and I was dancing and skating and everyone wanted me to help them and show them how to skate, I assisted a couple of them but then I got weary and had no fun while helping them and everybody were requesting me to tie their shoes because it's kinda tough to them since its their first time to skate. As usual I was with my three angels the whole time and teach them how to skate then we stood aside and chat and play with snow sprays and spray at each person passing next to us and then Jake bought me an energy drink since he knows that I'm in love with it. After a couple of hours of ice skating Mike, Jake and I went to play some billiard. On that day I really had fun with my three angels but my friends got mad at me because I didn't sit with them at all and then when I realized that I left them I went next to their table and no one even bothered to look at me, I walked away and stayed with 9th graders, I didn't get upset because I didn't want to ruin this incredible day.

28/march/2015

Dear Diary,

It has been a long time since I haven't wrote in my story, many things have happened to me that made me think of all the things that we have committed, sometimes life crashes you down but you should be strong enough to avoid it, you should stand up on your feet and say that I'm strong but I'm not like that, I really hope that I'm that strong and brave enough but there isn't any positive sparks in my head that encourages me to do that. The past few months, my life had been miserable, it was full of non-stop problems one after the other. I'm tired, I really wish that I wasn't a part of the problem or even thought of helping. My intension wasn't to ruin my sister's life, ok let me say it in an in-direct way. imagine; there was a hidden door that my sister wanted to know where is it, she used to tell that door had my name on it but I was 100% sure that it had her name on it, after a while I found the door and I showed her that it had her name, she liked it. Now, the key was left beside the door, I walked away and she tried to open that door with the key. she got inside and I got inside with her too and the key was left outside and the door got locked and we had no spare key, now we were afraid that anyone could open the door and see us inside with a third person. Did you understand what am I trying to say? The door was a man's heart, the key was the way to his heart, we both got into the trouble and were afraid to get caught, it might seem that's it's my fault but it's not, her intension at the first place was to try to open the door, no one forced her to do that but it isn't her fault too. It's like a puzzle; at last, someone did catch us and went into a huge trouble that had no ending. My only way to be happy was going to school and see my friends. I used to smile and laugh as much as I can because I knew that if I went home, it would be a disaster. People see me laugh and smile but they have no idea what I'm feeling and what's inside me. Sometimes I think in class and my friends ask me what's wrong, I wake up from day-dreaming and smile and say "nothing". Many people don't believe in black magic but in my religion we do, all of this happened because that man wanted to take my sister, actually he was a physco so he and his mother took her by black magic which affected me the most and my family.

CHAPTER 6

Time to study!

IGCSE is only a few months ahead and it time to study hard and leave all the fun for later on. 3 months before IGCSE I thought of my friends and that I will be leaving next year and will not see them for good and I don't want that to happen I can't stay away from my friends and I don't want to stay another year in this school and plus all of my friends are leaving so there is no use of staying and AS levels is damn tough for me, I can't handle it, I really prefer IB than British curriculum. This year I promised myself to study hard and leave everything behind and focus on my exams. My best friend Brooke has a really hard time in studying she has a difficulty in making a schedule and planning her time for studying, so I decided that let her come over a couple of weeks before IGCSE exams and I will help her study and explain her the difficult things that she doesn't know since that I have an idea of what our exam will be like. We both were excited and scared at the same time, IGCSE days were the most amazing days of 10th grade, Ms. Natalie went to India for her daughter's marriage and I really hope she has an amazing life and may god bless her, so the block was out of control though the student counselor and Ms. Uma were in charge of the students and still had no control on the students. The most thing that disturbed me was the problems that got more fierce and had really affected me but I tried my best to not think about it and study, I tried talking to Daniel since no one was there that I can talk to neither my sisters, I talked to him and told him everything inside me and about the problems that occurred the past few days and he really calmed me down and I felt relaxed that I had someone to talk to and let everything out of me, he told me not to worry and everything will be okay just focus on your studies that's the most important thing right now make your parents proud of you, at that moment I really felt lucky to have him and that I talked to him and he drew a smile on my face and changed my mood 360 degrees, I really don't know how to thank him I really owe him.

Day 1:

2nd may 2015

Tonight is the first night of Brooke sleeping over because we are going to study together for IGCSE and yes we are serious about it and hoping we'll get above C grade I really hope for the best. Brooke is a crazy person. With gods will we'll get up the next morning motivated!

We woke up the next morning and kept an alarm on 7:30 am but we were so tired that we couldn't even hear the alarm but we eventually woke up at 8:30. We woke with a smiling face, it's really an amazing feeling to wake up and look at your best friend sleeping right next to you, I woke her up and we had our breakfast and were definitely encouraged to study. We thought of studying physics and English today. We learnt some idioms that are necessary and well-read some formulas and concepts in physics. We naturally took some breaks and kept on watching at some videos on Instagram and vloggers on YouTube, she showed me something that really surprised me, there are vloggers actually Korean vloggers that make competitions in eating huge quantity of food like approx.

foodstuff that is enough for 20 people and they are literally so skinny and eat vast amount of food, I was just wondering where does all of these food go? I don't even see a change in their appearance. But it somehow disgusted me because while they are eating they talk to people online like video chats and they make irritating sounds while eating which I couldn't tolerate and Brooke was just laughing at my face expressions and when she laughs nothing can stop here. After our one hour break we started studying again till 5:00pm and then I started helping my mum with her orders, I haven't mention it but my mum has an online business on Instagram and she sell cakes and bites that are DELICIOUS I'm not saying that just because she's my mum I'm saying that because its 100% true and everyone admits it.

Day 2:
3rd may 2015

After a long night of studying we have our schedule planned and thought of studying different subjects tomorrow morning since that we have figured out that we have two exams on the same day ad both if the subjects are hard which is Mathematics 0580 paper 22 and Biology 0610 paper 6, I love alternative to practical they are actually the easiest paper even easier than multiple choice paper. Every day we hope the next morning would be better than yesterday!

BEEP BEEP *BEEP BEEP* the alarm keeps on buzzing and I could hear it while I was dreaming that happens to me a lot. We both woke up and had no interest in studying we were tired because we slept really late last night. We tried to freshen ourselves up a bit and started studying around 12:00. We went through Maths past papers and I asked her to answer the questions and ask me if she has any doubts. She filled some of the questions and I helped her answering the others, the problem in her is that she loses hope in herself at the first moment if she doesn't understand she calls herself "crazy" she's un-confident she doesn't know what she's capable of but I know that there is something much bigger inside her.

Day 3:

4ᵗʰ may 2015

Tomorrow is our first exam and we are dead frightened, we both were encouraging each other and telling that it's going to be easy don't worry but we are scared from the inside we were trying to ease each other.

We could feel butterflies in our stomach as fast as the time is getting late. Our first exam is English 0510 paper 21 and the timing was afternoon so we were fine with the timing, the only thing that got us scared is the writing part we should add some idioms to our writing which we suck at it. We searched for idioms that are mostly used on the internet and we wrote them down, we have our own way in memorizing stuff we make the situation funny so that we can remember it.

Day 4:

5ᵗʰ may 2015

Today is the big day! Our first exam is near! We woke up at 11:00 am to reach school early as what Brooke wants she always wants to get there early.

As shortly as we reached school we saw everyone looking so pale and terrified more than we are, this class makes me laugh, sometimes their fear is not at the right situation they keep on complaining about how nervous they are for the exam and are about to cry but 70% of their time is complaining and chatting and 30% of their time they are studying but I'm telling that they are not intelligent they are but not that much. We entered the exam hall and wished everyone good luck, all of us is staring at each other. I really thank god for the easy exam! I was answering the questions with a smiling face.

I should skip some of the days which nothing interesting happened except for continuous studying.

Day 7:

8th may 2015

Today is our English listening exam 0510 paper 41, it is on a Friday so I was at my grandmother's house in a family gathering I had my lunch and my uncle took me to school since that my dad was busy. Our exam starts at 3:30 but we all were gathered before time. No one was in school except for the security so we went to the kinder garden side and played in the playground.

Once I reached the school I saw my friends laughing so hard and I was asking them what's wrong what happened then they told me that they were playing the kids playground and they were taking videos in Snapchat. As usual Brooke is the first one to take videos of us and our funny moments we rode the swings and it was freaking scary they were taking it too high and all of them were laughing and screaming after that we fooled around and were damn thirsty we had no water to drink and it was hot, then we remembered that there is a water cooler inside the exam hall and we really thanked god in this condition. Our exam was easy but we had a problem in listening to the CD there was a lot of echo and the first two questions I could barely hear it and I left them because I didn't get to know anyone them even when it got repeated twice because the sound was low and a reverberation was there, but then it was good.

Day 10:

11ᵗʰ may 2015

The next day we had chemistry practical exam0620 paper 61, I usually love practical papers as I said but Brooke always had fear throughout her exams and while studying she always says negative things so while we were studying at the middle of the night, daddy came and told us why don't we study at Starbucks next to our school and then we can go school by walking, we stared at each other and like the idea but then Brooke pinched me and told me what if we had doubts what will do? I said we will think about it maybe next time.

As usual as we entered the class FEAR is all written on their faces and I get NEGATIVE VIBES! I hate the feeling that makes me feel that I haven't studied anything so I get out of the class and sit with my three angels they make my day better. All I have to say that this paper was EASY AS HELL! That really made me happy and satisfied about my exam.

Day 11:

12th may 2015

Our next exam is ICT 0417 paper 12, I HATE ICT! The problem is that last year in my IGCSE I didn't have ICT and no one helped me in studying all of this in less than 10 months, I couldn't understand anything and the teacher was only there for the first 3 months maybe and later o our Maths sir was teaching us but of course that's not it's job, our teacher left for some personal reasons and our school didn't bring a teacher only for our IGCSE practical! What about me?? I tried to ask some of my classmates how to study and what to study but still they don't have that much experience like a teacher does! I tried to self-study and took the help of YouTube but that didn't work 100% of the time, I really got troubled with this subject. Though, it was easy but really complicated.

Before we get to sleep we were watching vloggers on YouTube and that really made us feel like to try how they live and hold the cameras 24 hours and record their lives so, we decided the first thing we wake up we take a video of ourselves and while going to school so here we decided to go to Starbucks and study and record there. We ordered our drinks and sat and studied and it was empty the first moment we walked in because it was 7:00 am. We studied and then we went to the mall and recorded there and fooled around. A couple of hours before our exam we thought of going to school because it's a bit far and the weather was too HOT. So, we walked and while walking everyone were watching us and some of them beeping their horns at us, we were just snapchatting all the way to distract us that there is a long journey to reach to school as soon as we reached we were glad !

AFTER A LONG WHILE OF STUDYING AND PRESSURE...

FINALLY!! We are done with IGCSE exams! OMG I can't believe it I could literally cry right now. After 10 months of crying and hard work, this is day that I have been waiting for 10 months! To end this year and move on to the next level and a new school a new environment! And let me tell something better, SUMMER IS HERE!!

CHAPTER 7

The summer of my life

Writing a book is not that easy, you should add the exciting parts in your life but what I did is I added all the details of my daily life. Writing is my passion or you can say it's the cure to my wounds, it helps me to forget everything that has happened and get involved to typing while thinking, after that I have knew that I can write and really interested in this thing I started writing my book since last summer.

I hope this summer is better than the others.

Somehow I hate summer and love summer at the same time because I don't get to see my friends every day and I get to sleep late and wake up late which that is the most relieving part of summer. at the last day of school we planned to go to school on one of the Sundays so that we could sit together and see our friends so I talked to them on Friday because I got physcological problems again I started to cry when I first woke up, I really missed my friends I know it has just been one day but I miss them like it has been two years.

The first thing I thought of after ending my 10th grade is where will I go next? Which school? I always wanted to go to Abdulrahman Kanoo International School which my sister Beth graduated from, I wanted to join a different environment and go somewhere that encourages me to study and the main reason for choosing this school because they have IB diploma and most of the other schools have A-levels and AS-levels which I can't study that because it is very hard and that Is the reason that I don't want to go to my previous school. So I told my parents and I went to apply to for grade 11. I can't even believe that I'm even writing this "grade 11" finally.

Our trip to Thailand

Our first night at Thailand, Phuket, I don't have any words to define this remarkable and gorgeous country. The hotel is the furthermost hygienic hotel I have ever been in and their service is perfect and they are very generous. We are going to stay for just 3 days because we can't leave our business with no one handling it. Our suite had a private pool and we planned to wake up early morning to go to the swimming pool.

It is 8:00 am, and I put on my green swimsuit and hopped into the swimming pool, it sensed so energizing and comforting, it has been a long time since I haven't went swimming.

We had many plans for today, as soon as our parents woke up they had their breakfast and we went to have a quick bath and changed we went to the taxi and we could barely speak to the driver we talking with signals. So, we asked him to take us to Phuket beach. The waves were very strong and the sand was soft and warm as I fingered them running into my feet. All of the restaurants were serving only seafood and I hated seafood and I dislike its aroma but my dad was glad because he LOVES seafood particularly shrimp and crab, we were disgusted while watching him eating these creatures, so I thought of going next to the beach, I stood right at the beginning of the flowing waves

I liked the feeling of the sand underneath my feet getting soggy but when the water goes back I feel like tripping it happened twice and thrice so the fourth time I decided to stand and not hold myself from falling I wanted to see if I'm really going to fall or is it my imaginations, so I let myself free and the only feeling I got is the sand that smacked my face! I didn't even feel myself falling! I stood up and all of the people were giggling at me, I got covered with sand. I directly went and washed myself and sat with my dad, it's much better than getting humiliated in front of the people. Later on, we went back to the hotel because the waves were getting tougher and it's very hazardous and it's not permitted for people to be inside.

7:00p.m

We heard about a mall that is just 15 minutes away from our hotel it is called Jungcelon and it had many restaurants beside it and one of them was Pizza Hut, they have the most AMAZING pepperoni pizza! Despite the fact I'm not a fan of pepperoni but it was really delicious. The mall had many attracting things.

Second day at Thailand

We overheard that there is a place called Fantasia it's almost like a festival and has many facilities. I wore my black skinny jeans, my white Pink Floyd top, my black wedges and my black cap while my hair is blow dried and smooth down.

We rode the taxi and it's a long journey to go from the hotel to our destination. As we reached to our point, the place was huge! It was absolutely like a carnival, there were many animals like monkeys, fishes and butterflies. They even allow us to feed them, they gave us fish food and butter food and we paid for each about 50 Baht but it was worth it and we enjoyed feeding them especially the butterflies, they fly to the food that we held in our fingertips but somehow it was terrifying because there is a flying creature right on your hand which getting fed by you and I was stunned by their lively and bizarre wings, I have never seen a butterfly that close to me.

The monkeys were great too, they were hugging us and they loved me very much we gave them bananas and took a picture with them but one of the monkeys pulled Jade's hair and she started screaming and crying. We stayed laughing so hard at her. Then here was an elephant show, it was kinda boring because it wasn't that interesting and people were flying by strings and the elephants were dancing and the most frustrating part is that the show was silent.

Last day at Thailand

I can't believe we are leaving already but before leaving I want to have the best time I ever had in this wonderful country, too bad we just stayed for a couple of days because Phuket is a massive city and has several great places to visit but we ran out of time. So before I got to bed I scheduled what to do for tomorrow

Last Day At Phuket	
Time	**Plan**
7:00am	**Rise and Shine**
7:15-8:15am	**Swimming**
8:30-8:45am	**Quick Shower**
8:45-9:15am	**Get Ready and Leave**

9:20-11:20am	**Go shopping**
12:00-1:00pm	**Have lunch**
1:15-3:00pm	**Salon**
3:00-3:15pm	**Back to hotel**
4:00-4:30pm	**To the Airport**
5:30pm	**Departure**

One of the days of June

It's middle of the night and I'm on my bed writing while the lightning of my room is dim and I've been thinking of Brooke, the past 3 days she slept over at my house so tonight I'm unaccompanied I don't have anyone to talk to or irritate. Brooke Is the reason to my happiness, when she's around I'm always happy, she knows how to make me smile, angry, sad and irritate me. She understands me by just looking at her, she knows what I mean. She's crazy and loving. She asks me to massage her and then shouts at me that I don't know how to massage :$. You know, these little things make me laugh. While writing I remembered that my dad told me he will call Kanoo and ask them about my re test and if they said now, he will take me to the test! But I haven't studies yet! The most exciting thing is that Brooke will be with me "Inshalla"! We have nothing to do but pray for our IGCSE results! I'm starting to get tired and yawning and my head is aching really badly, haven't I mentioned that I'm having migraine? Oh well, I do. I had fun with Brooke today in fact every time with her is great. We were lying down on the bed and checking twitter and music covers while waiting for the time to pass by and then Turki came. This is the first time I mention him in this book, Turki is the son of my uncle who lives with us, which is my mum's brother, Turki is around 7 to 8 years old, I'm not sure but he is damn naughty and hits a lot, he is fun and annoying at the same time. Brooke and I were looking through old pictures of her and we laughed so hard because there is a huge difference and her poses are hilarious! The reason she left because she had to go to Julie and Julia since they are leaving at the end of the month back to Egypt and maybe 10% possibility if coming back. Julie and Julia are non –identical twins, they are Brooke's childhood friend and three of them came together to our school so, this year they became my classmates and they were my bus mates too.

These two people are really precious, I really adore them and they are very respectful I even met their parents they are very welcoming and especially their adorable mom. I just went to their house twice and the first time I went was like I am a regular visitor that really made me feel comfortable and welcomed. I really loved their mom and I hope they continue their life incredibly at Egypt.

29ᵗʰ June 2015

Around 4:00 a.m.

Daddy is going to Saudi now to take my aunty and my cousins to my grandmother's house; they are going to stay for the rest of Ramadan². My little sister Jade really tested my temper today; she annoyed me with her cocky attitude. I don't know why she does that. So, tomorrow after Iftar we are going to keep henna for a special occasion that is held

---

² A month where all muslims fast

at the 15th of Ramadan, which is named by "Girgaoun[3]", I thought of making like Demi Lovato's tattoo "Stay Strong" well maybe I'm not sure.

My second night without my love L

I miss her already!

If you waited for something you want really bad, it will look like it a decade, but if it's not constantly in your head it will pass by like draining water. Kanoo is my only concern these days; I really want to go there! I don't want to come back to that school, it will make me feel sick plus the school looks dead, everyone is leaving. I have a fear, which what makes me write before I get to sleep, because it makes me tired and sleep like a baby. I guess that's the only thing that I won't share in this book because it's complicated and I can't explain what my fear is. It's not phobia or anything; it's from what I have experienced the past few months.

---

[3]   An occasion where kids collect sweets and nuts just like trick or treat

I'm in love…!
I always think about you,
And wonder what you are doing,
And what you want to do.

I think about how much I love you,
But you don't think about me,
That's what makes me crazy.

I think about how much I wanna see you,
And see your irresistible eyes,
This makes me feel abnormal.

I think about how much I wanna be with you,
I want to tell you that I love you,
But I'm afraid your answer won't be "I love you too"
-Meme

30ᵗʰ June 2015

5:?? am

Today was maybe the worst day of this month. While I was praying at 7:15 pm, I heard mommy and Beth shouting, I wondered, "what now!!" I went and their voices kept on going louder, why? Before that Brooke whatsapped me saying, "Meme, hello" I replied and the first thing she sent was, "Kanoo didn't accept me" I got confused, I asked her how and she told me everything, I really got sad and it ruined my mood. Then she told me she won't come tomorrow to my house because our classmates are invited to one of our friend's house and she says that it's the last hangout with Julie and Julia since they are leaving. I said fine. Two shocks in a row. Then mommy and Beth didn't talk to each other, we were supposed to go to keep henna and meet our aunty and cousins that just arrived from Saudi but none of these happened because mummy got really mad at Beth. After hours of convincing Beth to help Mommy to say sorry, she went and everything got back to normal. We sat all together and watched our daily series. Then later on at 1:00 am Kate talked to me and we chatted then she told me that my classmates planned a gathering at city Centre at 1st of July. I told Brooke if she is going or not because she was supposed to come to my place and celebrate Girgaoun, she told me no I can't come and gave me her same excuse, "as you know Julie and Julia are travelling on "6th JULY"! I won't be able to see them, I hope you understand". I really got pissed off because it's the second time she ditches me! I ignored her and she tells me don't ignore me, I told her, "I was busy…" that's it, then around 4 we played "Bahraini deal" with mummy and Jade which changed me mood into better.

I need you…!

4th July 2015
6:00 am

I couldn't write the past couple of days since I used to get in bed tired as hell. The thing that I want to add is; at the 1st of July which was Girgaoun, it was literally AMAZING. We had a lot of fun and danced a lot, many kids came and we sang for them and some kids came for us too but our cousins were the best, a bunch of boys came with a huge speaker with traditional songs and four of them were dancing and we were clapping with huge smiles on our faces. Then my aunty danced and I couldn't handle myself from not dancing though my parents and all of them were there but when there is music "Meme forgets who is around and starts to shake it" I couldn't describe that day everyone had fun I will never forget this special day

Tomorrow we are having a family hangout, all of us will be there our cousins my aunty and my parents, we were supposed to go tonight but we couldn't it was last and plus everyone were tired. I hope tomorrow will be better.

Never lose hope…

7th July 2015

8:00 am

We went to my grandmother's house around 12:15 am and before that my dad came and when I was about to get out from my room, Jade came running saying, "don't come out, Daddy came with a man"

"A man?!" I replied confused.

I waited for daddy to come to the room and I asked, "Daddy who did you bring with you?"

He replied, "Jay".

My face reaction was ":/"

What brought him here? Oh! I didn't tell you who Jay is. He is my cousin from Saudi well actually his name is John. So, I changed and went to him with my sisters. We were chatting about money and then all of a sudden he says, "Meme, I want to go to Germany" and I was like in a sarcastic way, "come on lets go". But he was serious he really wanted to go, we convinced him, we told him, "you have a monthly salary, save them for just two months and its more than enough for two weeks at Germany." Then we planned to go next summer with Beth, Helen, Zedd, Jay and I. we will save money till next year and travel, we encouraged him and he got really happy.

We went to my grandmother's house and we sat all together and felt hungry so we all stared at each other and gave an evil smile we all understood what we meant, we wanted to order food so it was around 1:30. We ordered from "Burger Line" it has the most delicious grilled burgers ever!

A few minutes later...

Jay and my uncle were arguing about something that happened today, I couldn't anything but two voices yelling, then Jay started to raise his voice at him and my uncle is very to annoy and test him temper and the first thing he does; he hits. So, when Jay started being a brat and doesn't watches out for what he says, my uncle ran to him and starts to hits him, then they calmed down a bit and Jay starts once again to shout, so my uncle took his belt out and beat him and thanks god nothing serious happened and if it wasn't for my dad and his um he wouldn't stop hitting otherwise Jay would have been dead right now.

After 2:30 my mum was so tired so she said as soon as our food arrives we take it and eat it at home. My mum gets really tired because she has thyroid problems and blood pressure she can't stay in hot conditions and a place with noise. We got sad because we won't get to eat with our cousins and we tried to convince her to stay a bit more, we are playing a losing game.

I miss you...

8th July 2015

7:58 am

As I woke up around 5:45 pm, I went to wash my face and prayed as o finished I heard mummy talking to my aunty Sawsan and she was speaking in a worried voice, I was curious and wanted to know what is happening, the only thing that I heard was my dad's name, my aunty Jameela and my grandmother, then when I was watching T.V, Beth came and told me what happened, well it is a problem that has no ending, family problems that we are sick and tired of. The thing that I'm really worried and annoyed about are my hands, remember when I kept henna, I kept black henna and I have a sensitive skin so it was itching me and I kept on scratching it until I realized that my hands are totally red and infected.

OMG... I'm dying its itching me really bad!! I shouldn't scratch it!! It will be worse! Ugh!!! Its hurts…

Its 9:47 a.m.

And I'm waiting for my uncle Christopher to come and take me to the hospital. I've been waiting since 1 hour and 15 minutes. I'm really scared, I'm afraid that it will remain as it is because the henna is literally drawn on my hand. I've seen a lot of people that had the same thing that I do right now but I never thought that one day will come and it will happen to me and I've seen pictures on Google too sometimes when I search for black henna on images, these disgusting pictures appear that I can't handle looking at!

10:59a.m

I just came back from the hospital, the just gave me a cream to apply twice daily and pills. They told me that they can give me an injection but it's not that infected. I was really worried so directly as I came back I slept.

I kept on waking up a couple of times because it itch me a lot

Can't forget you...

THIRD AUGUST 2015!!

Today is the big day. It's my birthday and I'm finally turning 16! I have to wake up early to get ready for my hangout with my best friends. I kept my alarm at 10:00a.m to rise and get to the Salon.

BEEP BEEP BEEP BEEP

Its 10:00a.m

I jumped out of bed and washed my face; I wore my Adidas tracksuit and my Nike shoes and off to the hair salon. I was smiling all the way and was damn excited. I wanted to make something different today, so I dyed my hair light brown and blonde highlights that made a stunning combination and now it is time for my hairstyle! I thought of making big beachy waves since my hair is very full. I've done my manicures and pedicures and now it's time for SHOPPING!

I went to City Centre Mall and firstly started to window shop but then I kept on mind that I don't want something too fancy and neither too simple, I want something that describes me. So, I went to many shops but the only shop that

I stood right in front of it with my mouth open wide saying in my thoughts that that's the perfect dress for today! I went inside and stared at that stretchy long sleeves black mini dress that has stripped Swarovski crystals under the chest, it was PERFECT! And next to it was that plain matte white heels that is 4 inches high and the crochet bag that is filled with Swarovski crystals and it was my lucky day, they had a mega sale and it was 60% off and I couldn't handle myself from not buying it, I took all of it and didn't mind about the price. I called the driver to come and pick me up from the mall and take me home but while waiting I got myself some frozen yoghurt that I'm ADDICTED to.

I reached home around 12:55 and directly went to my room and prepared everything. For the makeup I applied:
-Contour
-Soft pink blusher
-Mascara from Max Factor
-Matte red lipstick from Mac *That I LOVE*
I wore my dress and my heels, as I looked at myself through the mirror, the only things that came out of my mouth were, "WOW!" I looked gorgeous. As I came down the stairs my

parents saw me and they glaring at me with a beautiful smile drawn on their faces, I hugged them and kissed them and they told me, "Happy Birthday my Angel". I felt like crying but I was afraid to ruin my makeup =).

I hopped on to the car and texted my friends, "I'm on my way xo". It took me 25 minutes to reach to the restaurant and I was right on time! As I entered the restaurant, the waiter took me to our table and my friends were waiting for me with huge smiles on their faces and wrapped gifts all over the table. I hugged them with tears in my eyes. We laughed and talked a lot and ate a lot too but we really had a lot of fun. They got me many presents, Brooke got me a Versace dress, Kate got me Louis Viton heels, Rebecca got me Nike jordans and its my dream shoes and Rose got me Armani perfume, she knows I love Armani. All of the gifts were wrapped with green! My favorite color! I really thanked them a lot and I didn't know how to!

After our lunch has ended they told me that they have prepared for me a surprise and as I entered the limousine that they rented for me, they will blind fold me. "I can't even believe they rented me a limousine, that's way too much :')"

We got out of the restaurant and all of them were waiting for me next to the limousine, with my smile on my face and as I'm walking towards them, I heard a gentle voice behind me whispering, "Happy Birthday My love" my heart raced, this voice was very familiar, with every second as I turn around my heart raced faster and faster and as I saw him right in front of me, I wanted to give him a huge tight hug but he did, he hugged me. I miss his adorable hugs that made me feel safe whenever he grabs me and at that second my eyes started to shed with tears and my heart was pounding. Finally It's him, the guy that I loved and cherished for years, the guy that whenever I used to chat with, always drew a smile on my face, the only guy that I trusted in my whole life, the guy that made me stronger and made me have hope in everything that broke me down, the guy that lifted me up in my downs, the guy that fought for everything just to make me happy and be with me, the guy that made me smile the moment I firstly saw him, he is the one that made me understand what LOVE means, Do I like him? No, I love him. Why do I miss him? I haven't seen him for more than a year. Yes, I love him with no fear, I love him with all my heart. It's him that I have been mentioning earlier he's the guy that I fell in love with, he is the guy that I miss, he's the guy that I can't forget and never lose hope in our love. I miss staring at his light brown eyes and his beautiful smile, I miss when he used to tell me "I love you", I miss our little memories that we had together, I miss when he used to get jealous, I miss when he used to stare at me with love in his eyes...

I really can't believe my eyes; he's right in front of me!

I can't believe it is Cooper!

To be continued...

Poems Written By Me;

WITH TRUE EMOTIONS AND MEMORIES

12/8/14

Tortured? No

Disappointed? No

Depressed? No

But broken, missing, over-thinking

EXPLOSION!

Boom…

Everything exploded

Everything got broken down,

I'm out of ideas…BLANK

Don't know what to do…CONFUSED

Would anyone bother to help me?

Haha of course not

They think its wrong…

I'm still just a kid that's what they say

Ok, I'm done with people saying what they had to say; now it's my turn

It's my turn to say what's hidden inside

Every human being has feelings right?

Connections happens,

Hormones get active,

Here where love happens.

Age is just a number

But true love…

Nothing can stand in its way

Two people fight for their love

They survive together

Stand together,

Help each other through their hardest times

Care...

They care for each other,

They want to be together,

Stay together and love together

I don't care how old am I

I got blind and love gets you blind

I have my limits,

Everything has limits.

Why should you separate two people that truly love each other?

Don't say we are kids!

We are mature enough to love to take responsibility of what we are doing,

We know what's right and what's wrong

We are in love and no one can get in our way!

26/6/2013

You've been with me through my saddest and happiest times,

Sometime we fight but I always kept on my mind that you

were mine,

And that you were worth a thousand dime,

I loved you for who you are,

And since that day onwards, you refused to exit my mind,

I kept on dreaming and thinking about you again and again,

And when I miss you, I could feel the pain inside my vein,

Don't forget that you drive me insane!!

25/6/2013

A lot of bullshit on my mind right now,
Don't know what to say or what to do,

Should I spill it out or,
Just sleep and forget about every shit?,

Tired and I'm out of words!,
Don't want this day to end,

But it's not in my hands,
Shut my mouth with some band?,

Or fill my brain with sand?,
I just want a magic wand,
To send me to a crazy land!

14/9/2013

Did I get the right person?,
Or did I just forget how to defend?

It's all matter of time,
To get back and smile,

You fell and told you're fine,
I held you and took you too high,

Made you feel happy with pride,
After a while,
You left me aside,

It took me years and years until I tried to survive,
But I couldn't,
My heart failed to live,

Missing you was like burning me alive,
As soon as I die,
I don't want you to come back and cry !

26/11/2013

You still stare,

But I don't care,

I can't bare the pain,

I stood right there and started to cry under the rain,

Seriously, what did you gain?

Living with no worries,

And no love stories,

But I can't say No,

To the person that I adore,

No it's not over,

You can't leave your lover,

That would be rude,

But hey dude! I realized that you just did,

And that was painful,

One more tear and I'm gonna crash you into the wall,

And gonna let you fall from the 3rd floor,

And going to go out of that DOOR!,

I'm sure you're wondering which door?

It's definitely the door of my life.

UNKOWN DATE

Sometimes,

There is this moment where I just stay there and think,

Think about my past and what have I done to make it sink,

I talk to myself a lot, figuring out what are my mistakes and
how to correct them,

But sometimes, there is something that stops in my way and
I fail to understand what it is,

Until I grab my paper and pen, write my thoughts and what's
inside my head,

I lose my confidence and hope, I say that I can't and mislead,

All of these negative points comes inside me and brings me
down,

And then they keep on wondering why I look at them and
frown,

No one was there to lift me up or at least give me a hand,

Everyone left me alone and didn't care about this girl whose suffering everyday and wouldn't sleep until her pillows are soaked with tears,
No one even knows what my biggest fears are,

But it's alright; I'll be stronger and confident build up my personality and be the best.

24/12/2014

I love your voice,

I love your eyes,

I love your smile,

When I look at you all the time,

You make me feel fine,

That's why I think you are kind.

I start to stare,

But I guess you don't care,

And what I can't bare,

Is your attractive hair.

The way that you look at me,

Makes me feel I'm your enemy.

I really don't know what you have done to me,

But I guess that's how it's suppose to be.

I have many questions inside my head,

And I don't think that it should be said,

I'll wait until it fades away day by day.

Printed in the United States
By Bookmasters